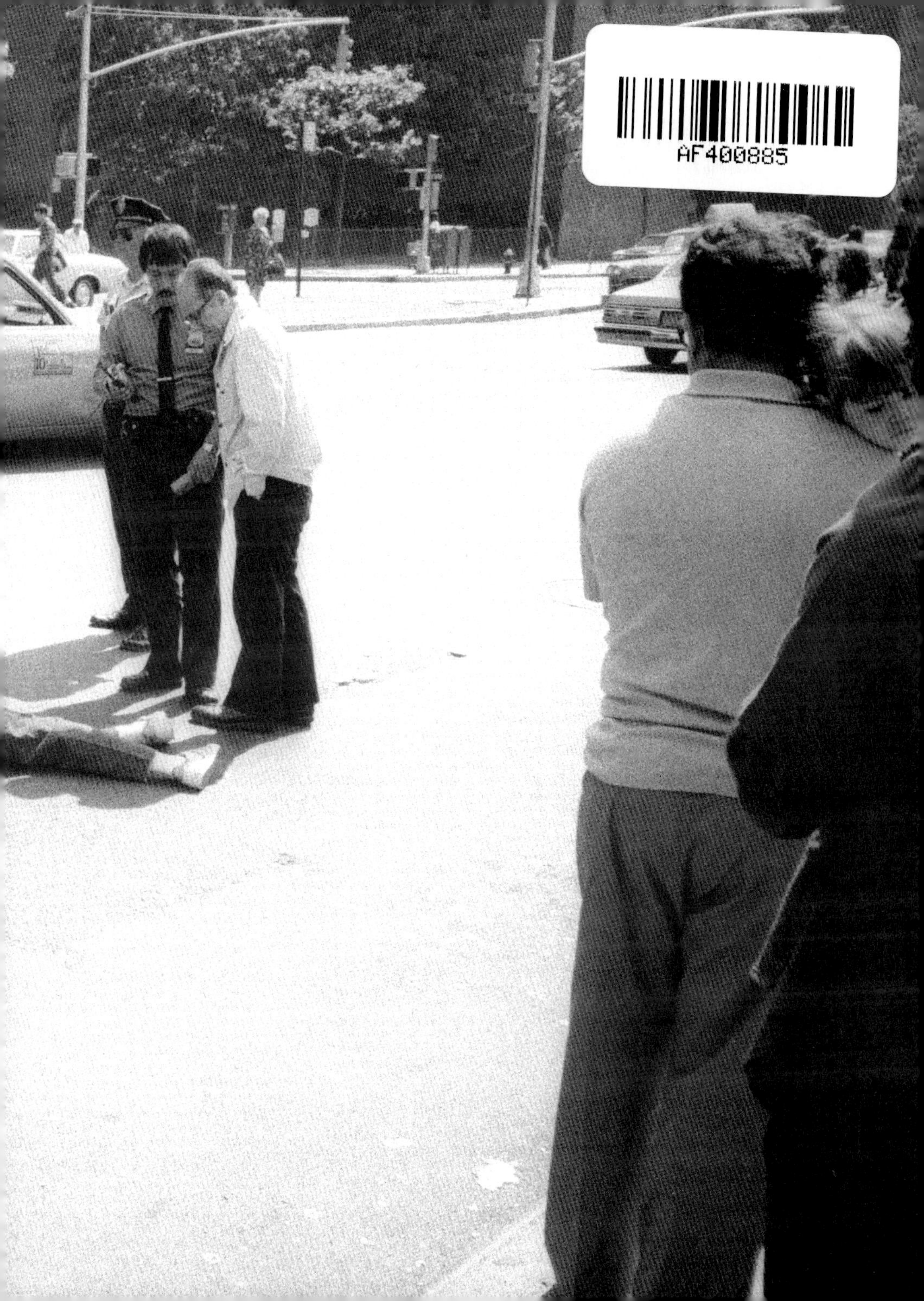
AF400885

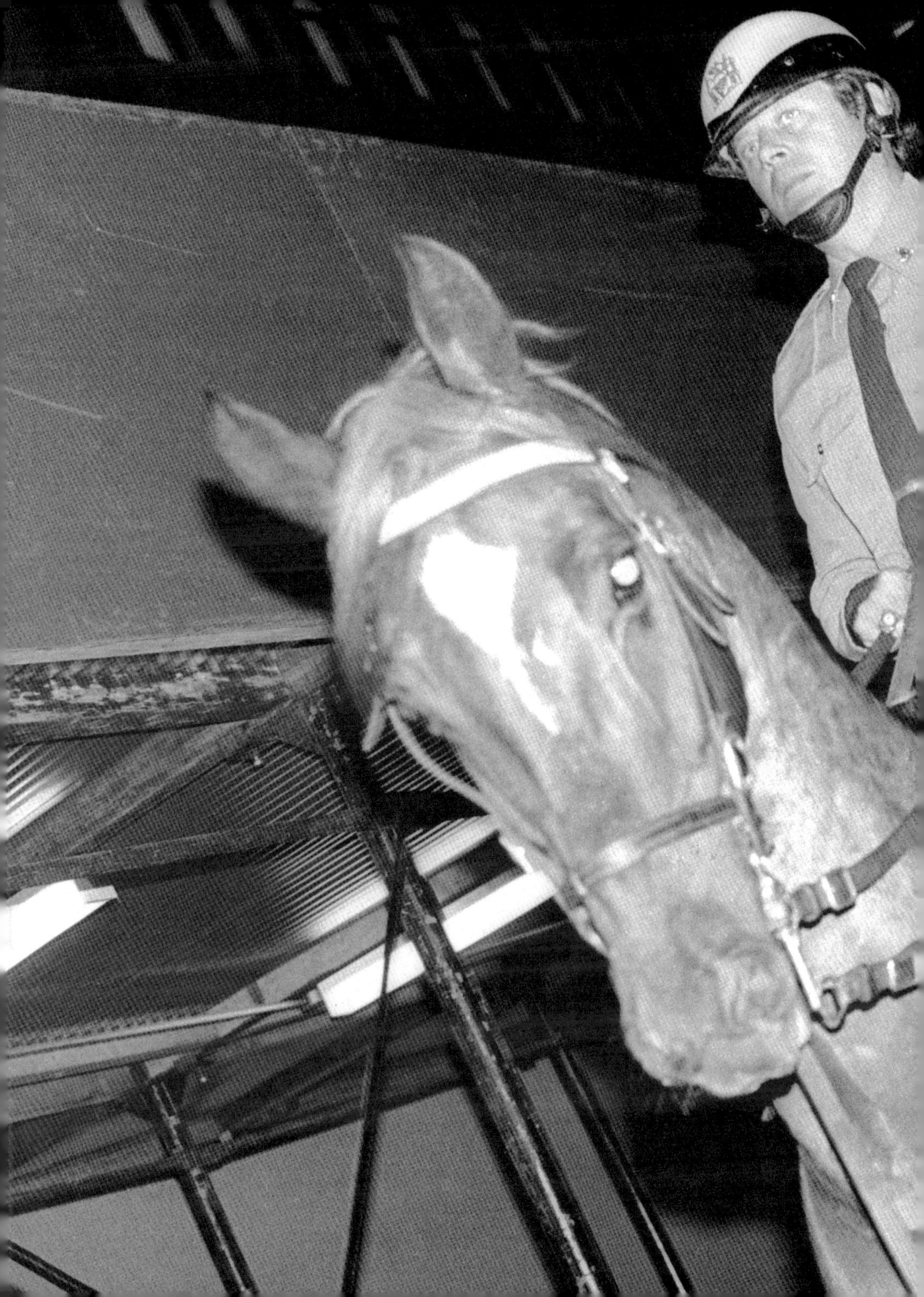

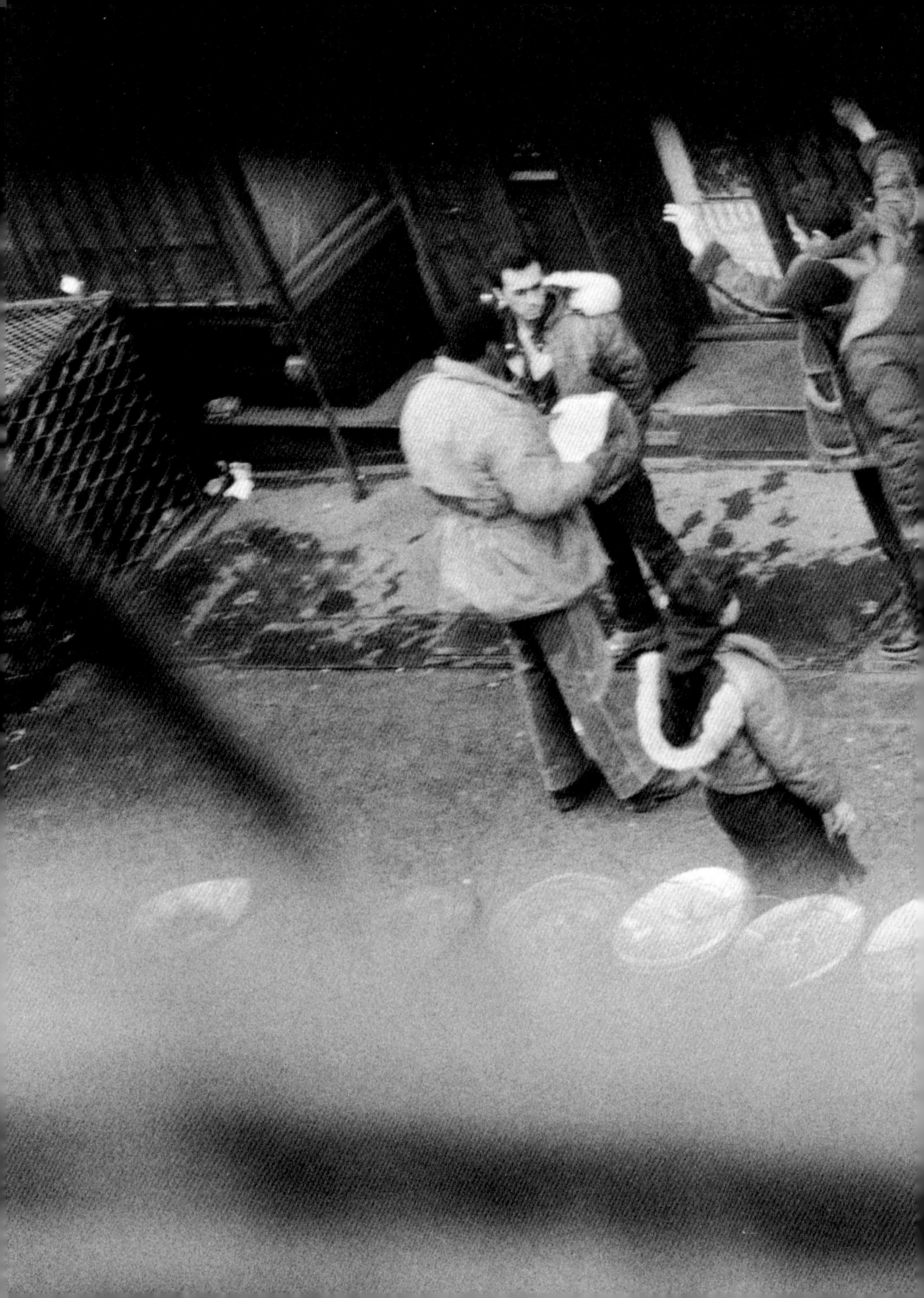

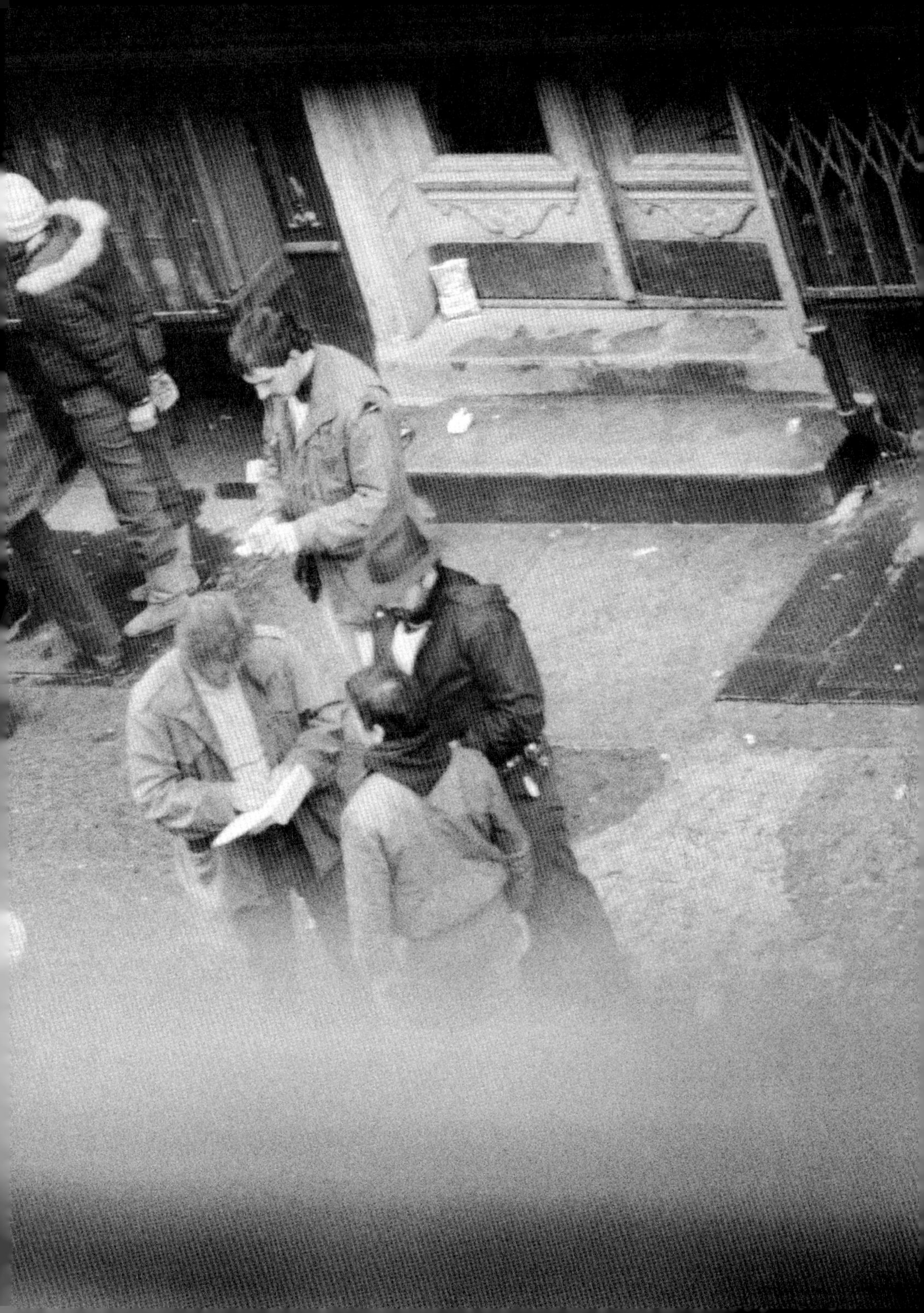

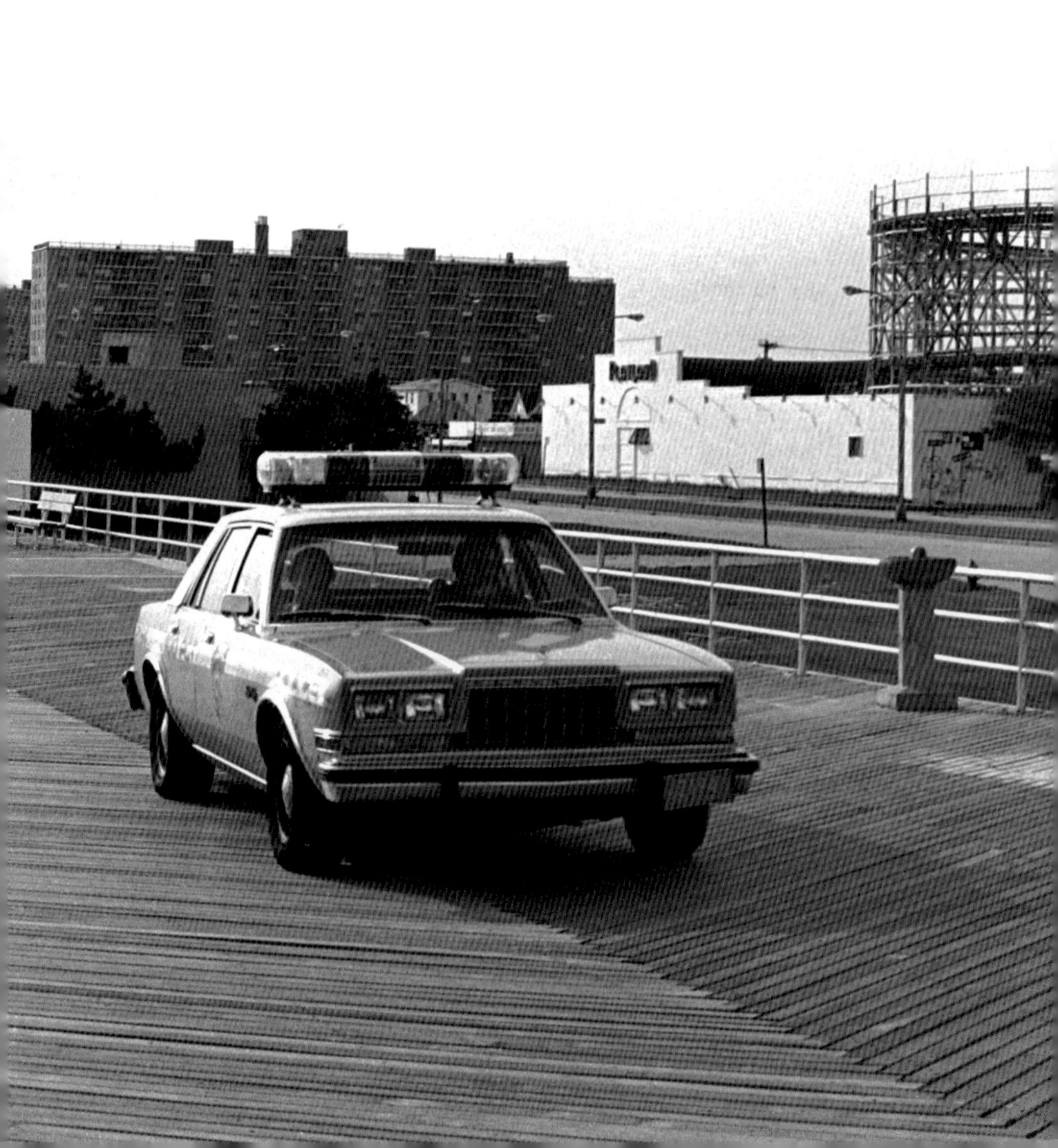

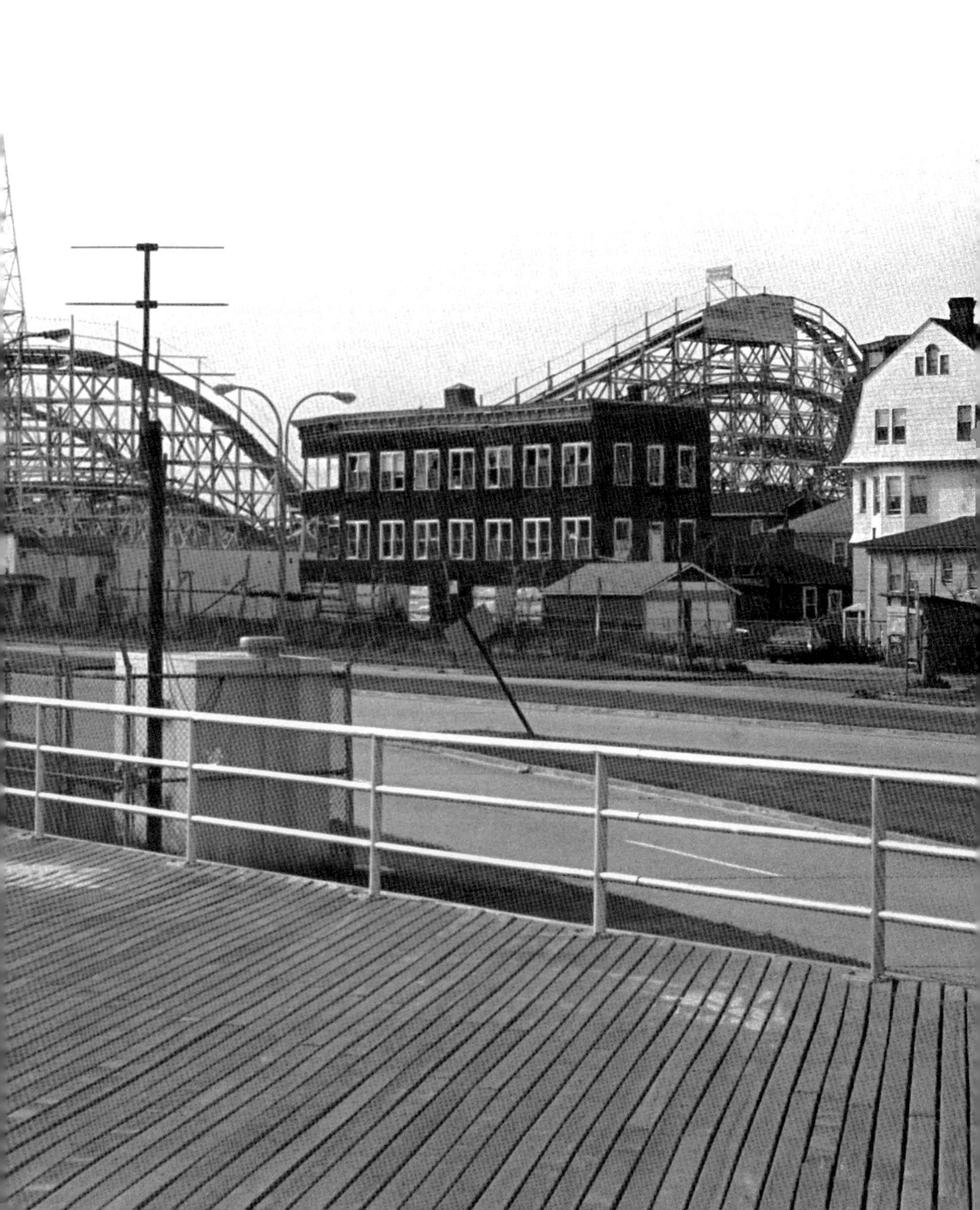

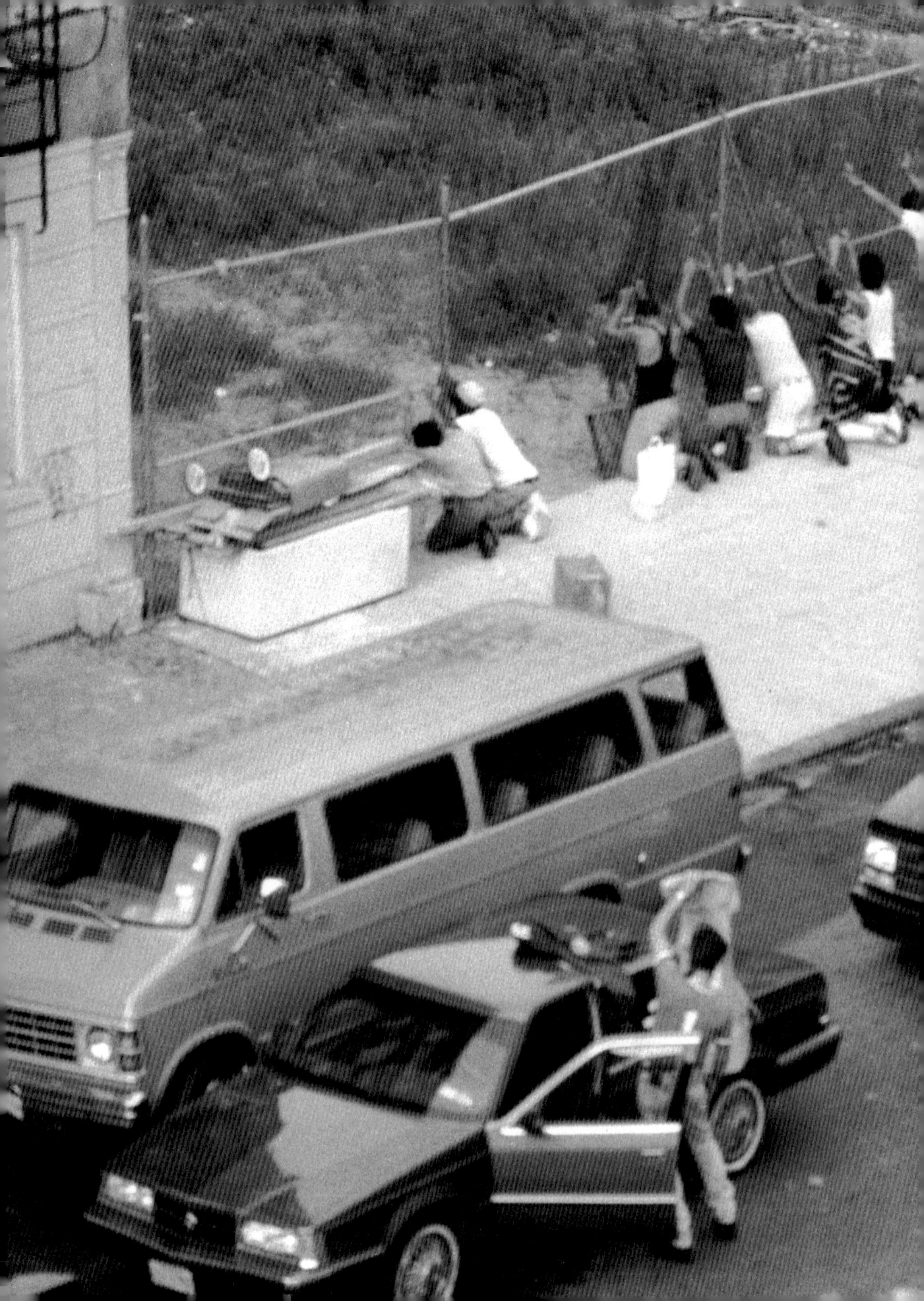

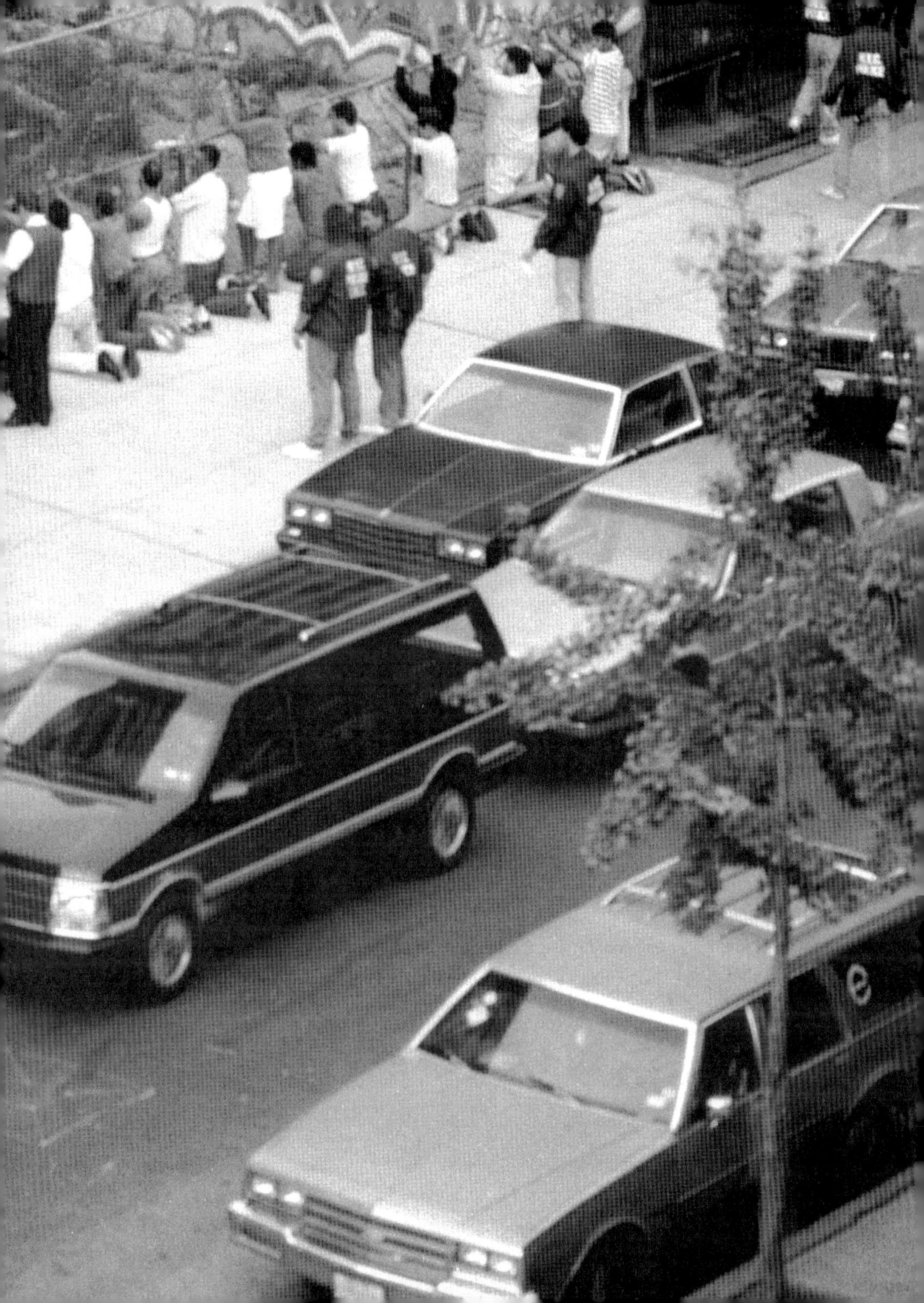

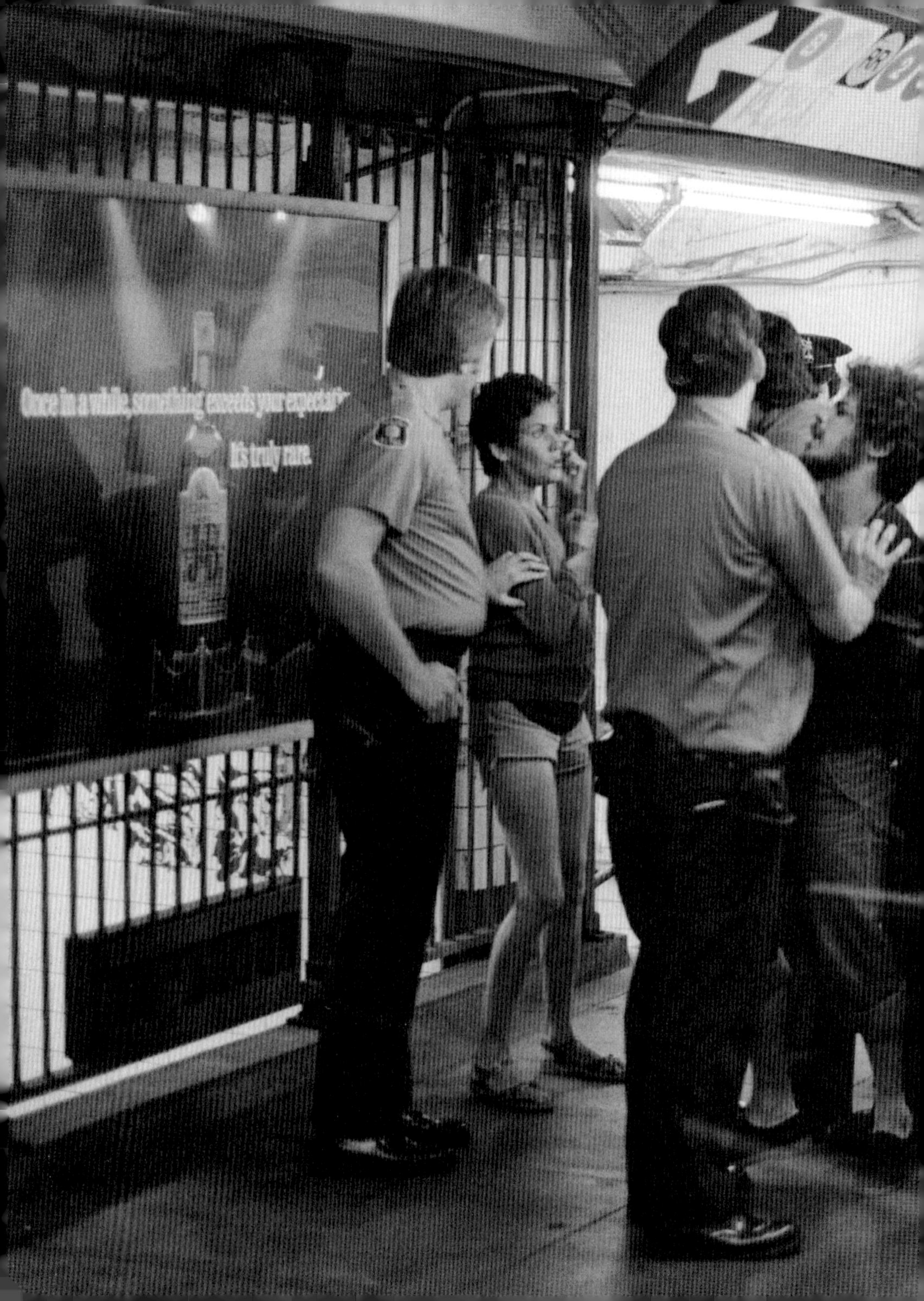

Once in a while, something exceeds your expectations.
It's truly rare.

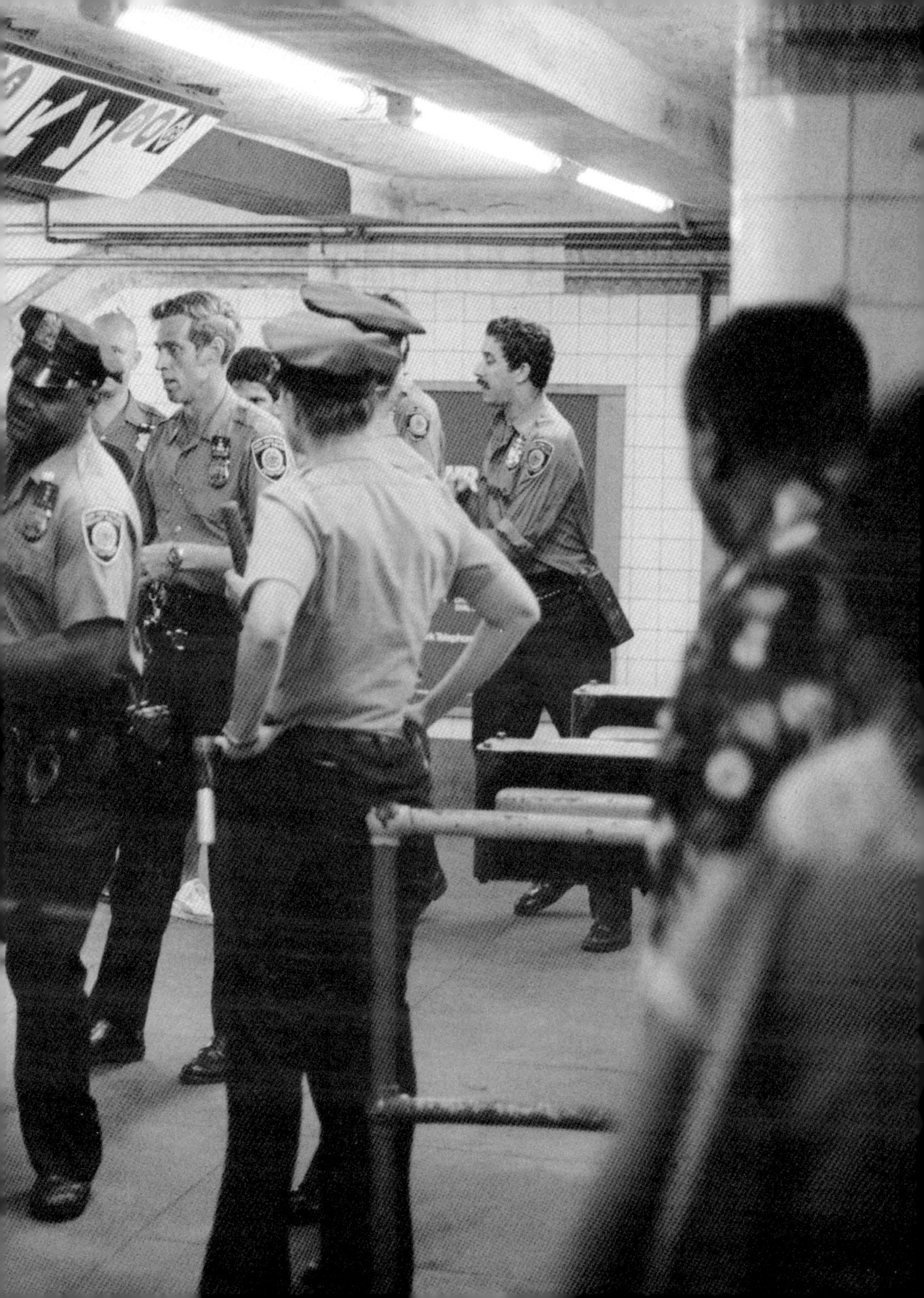

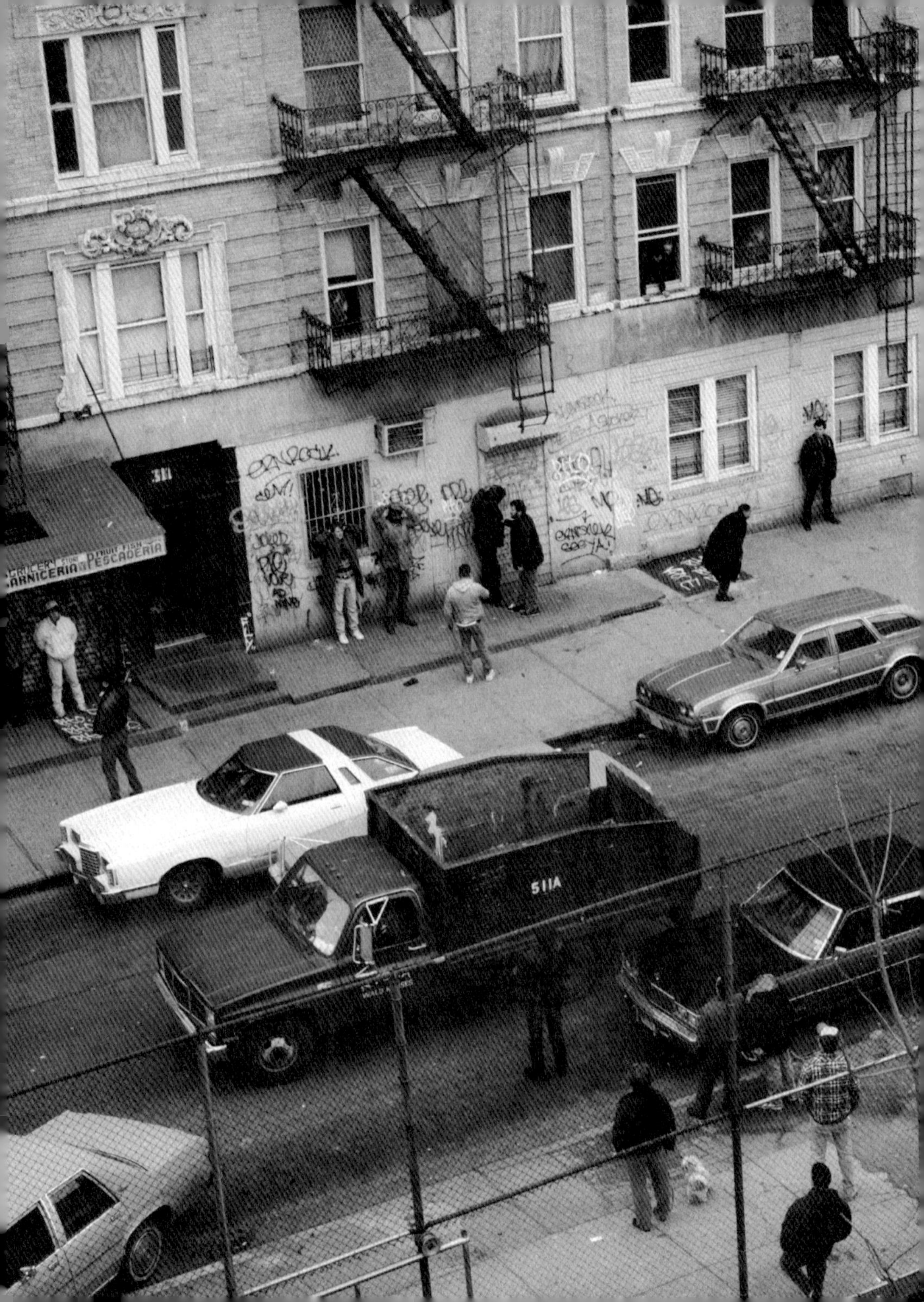

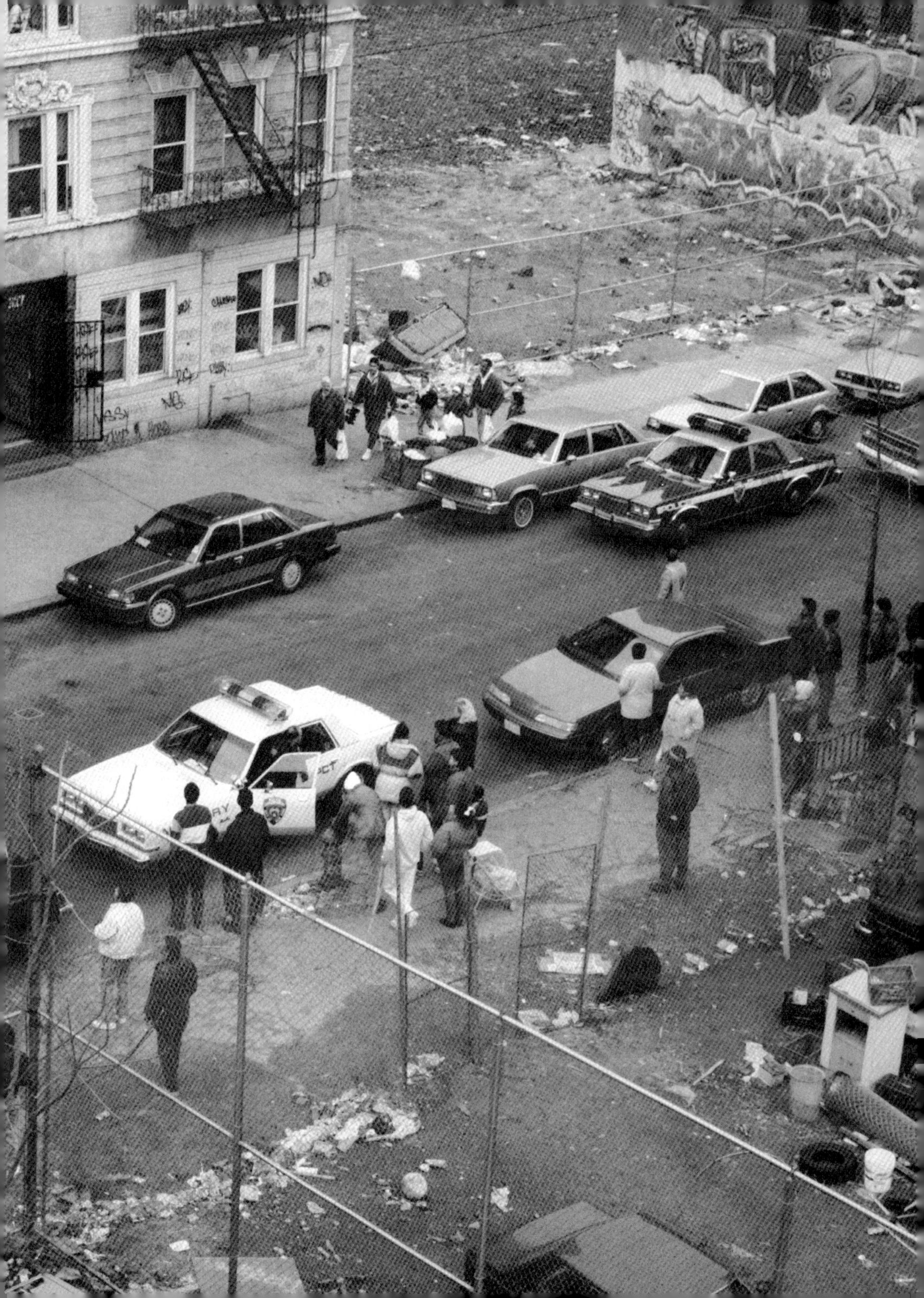

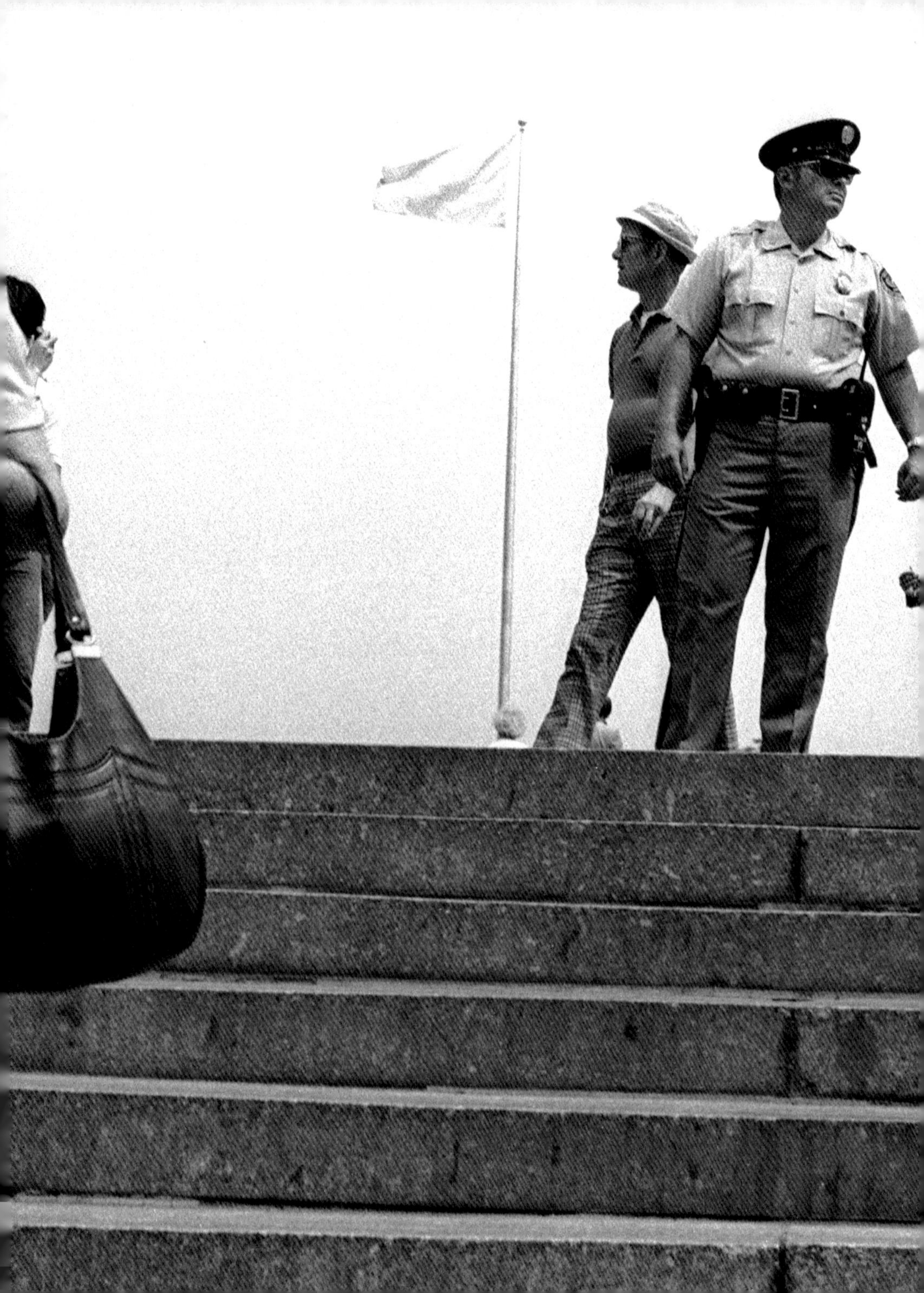

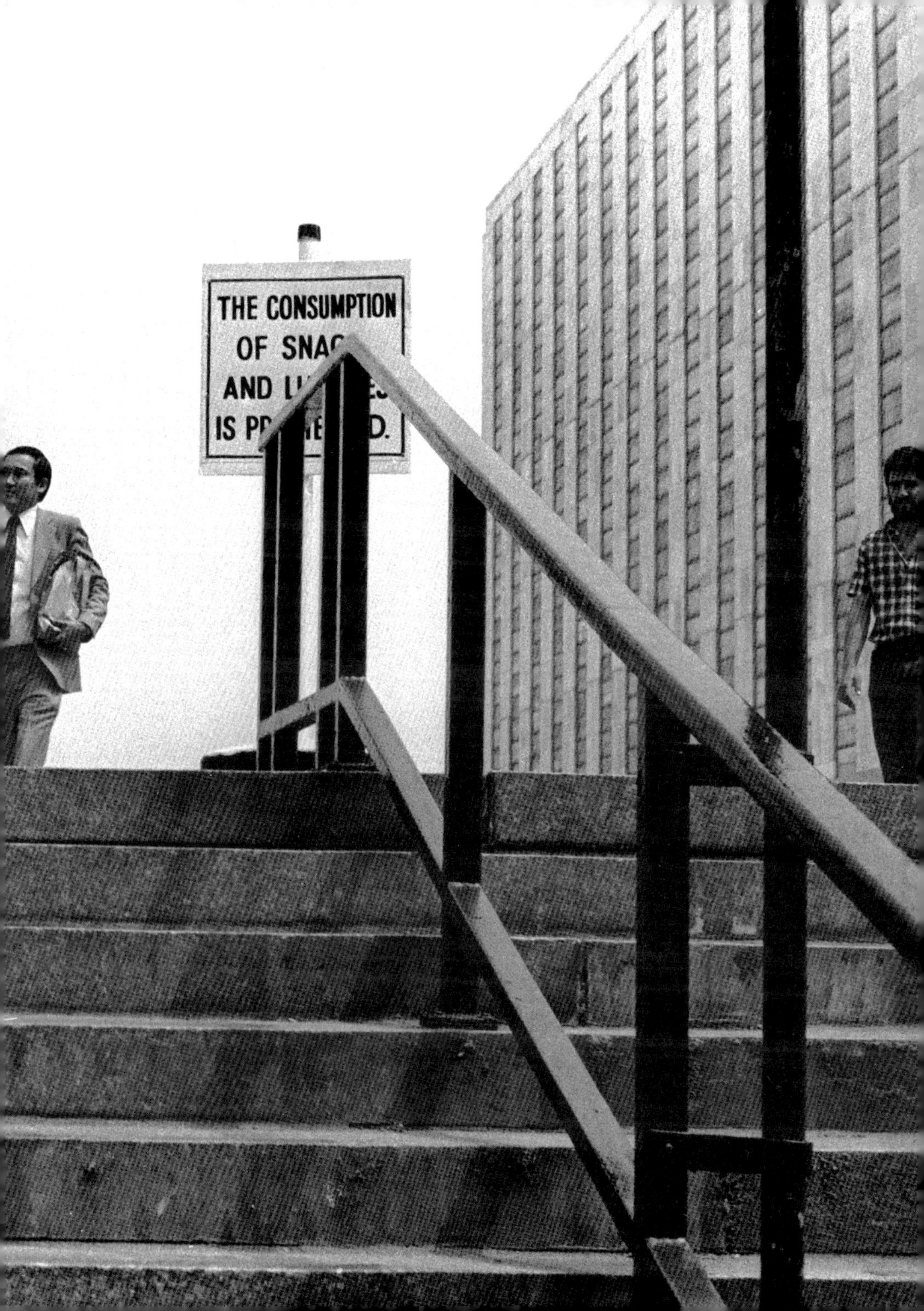

THE CONSUMPTION
OF SNACKS
AND LUNCHES
IS PROHIBITED.

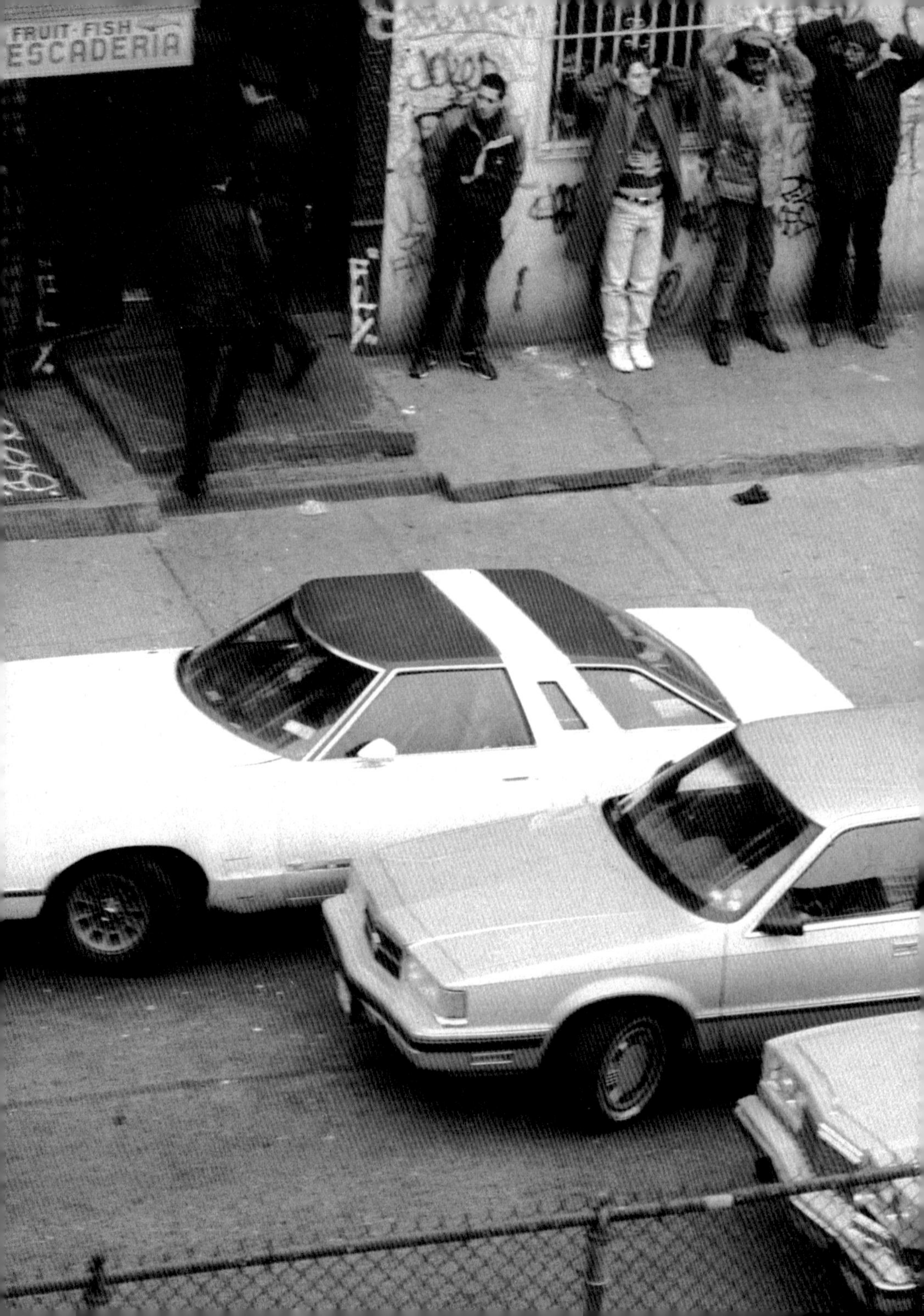

FRUIT·FISH
ESCADERIA

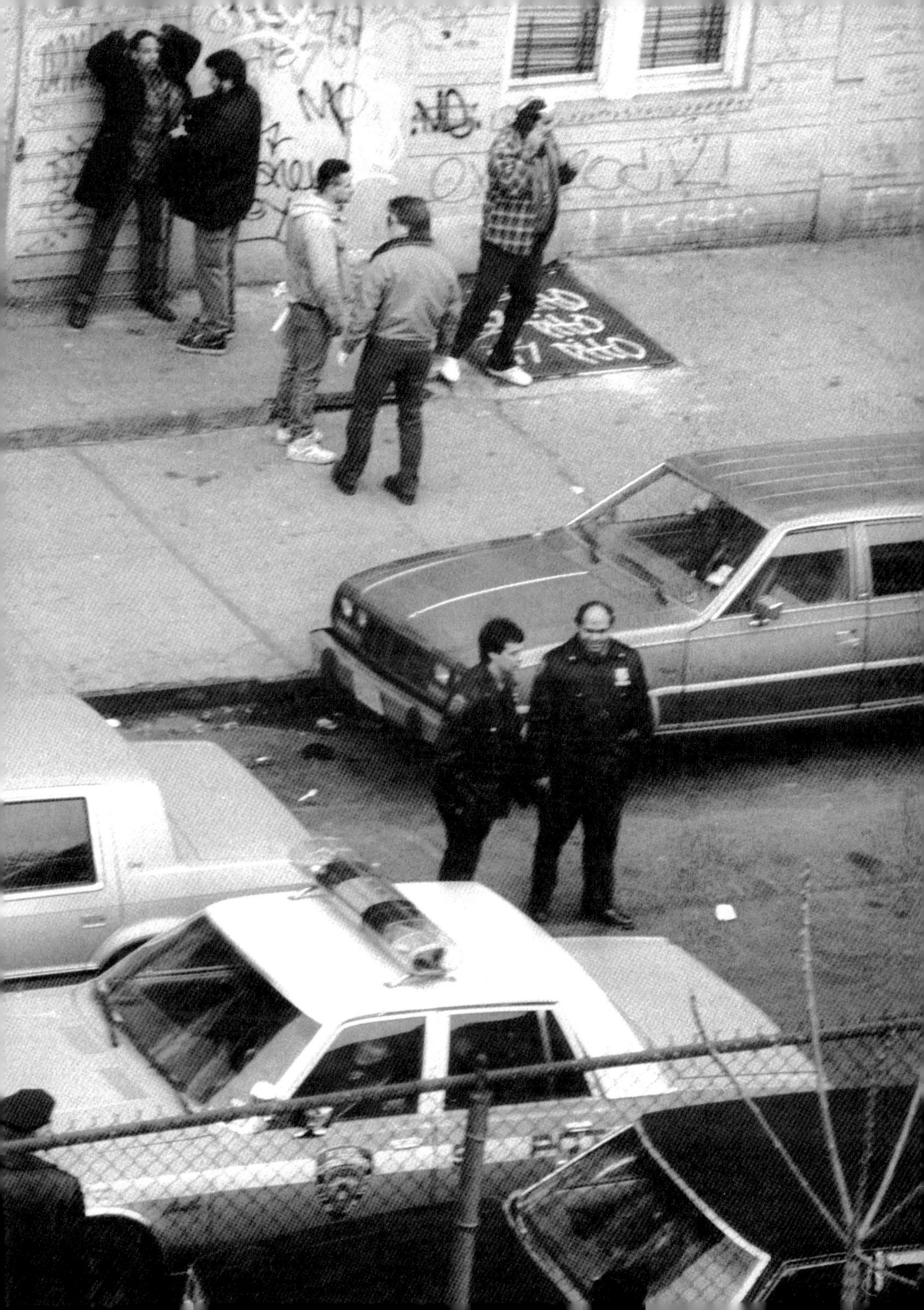

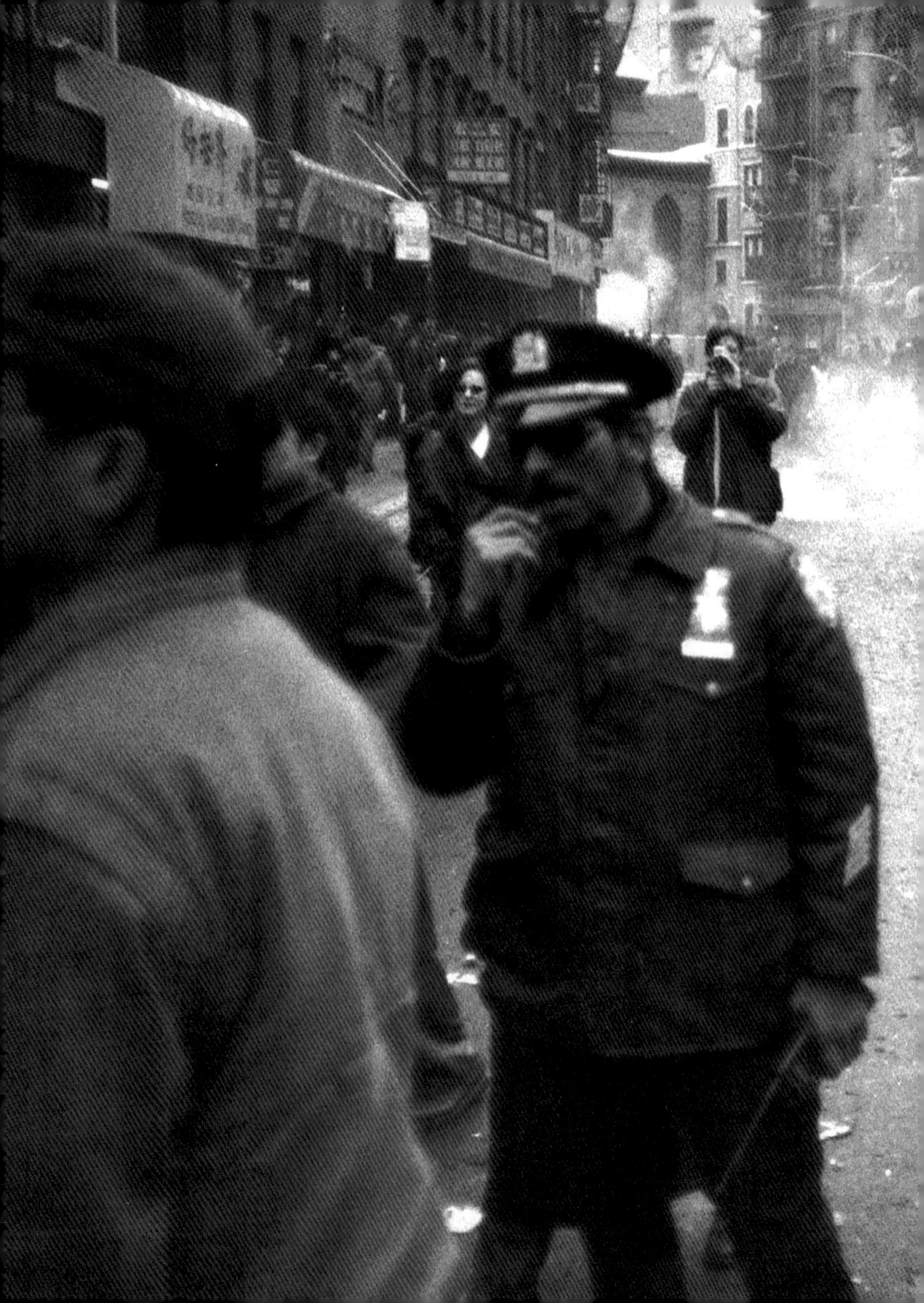

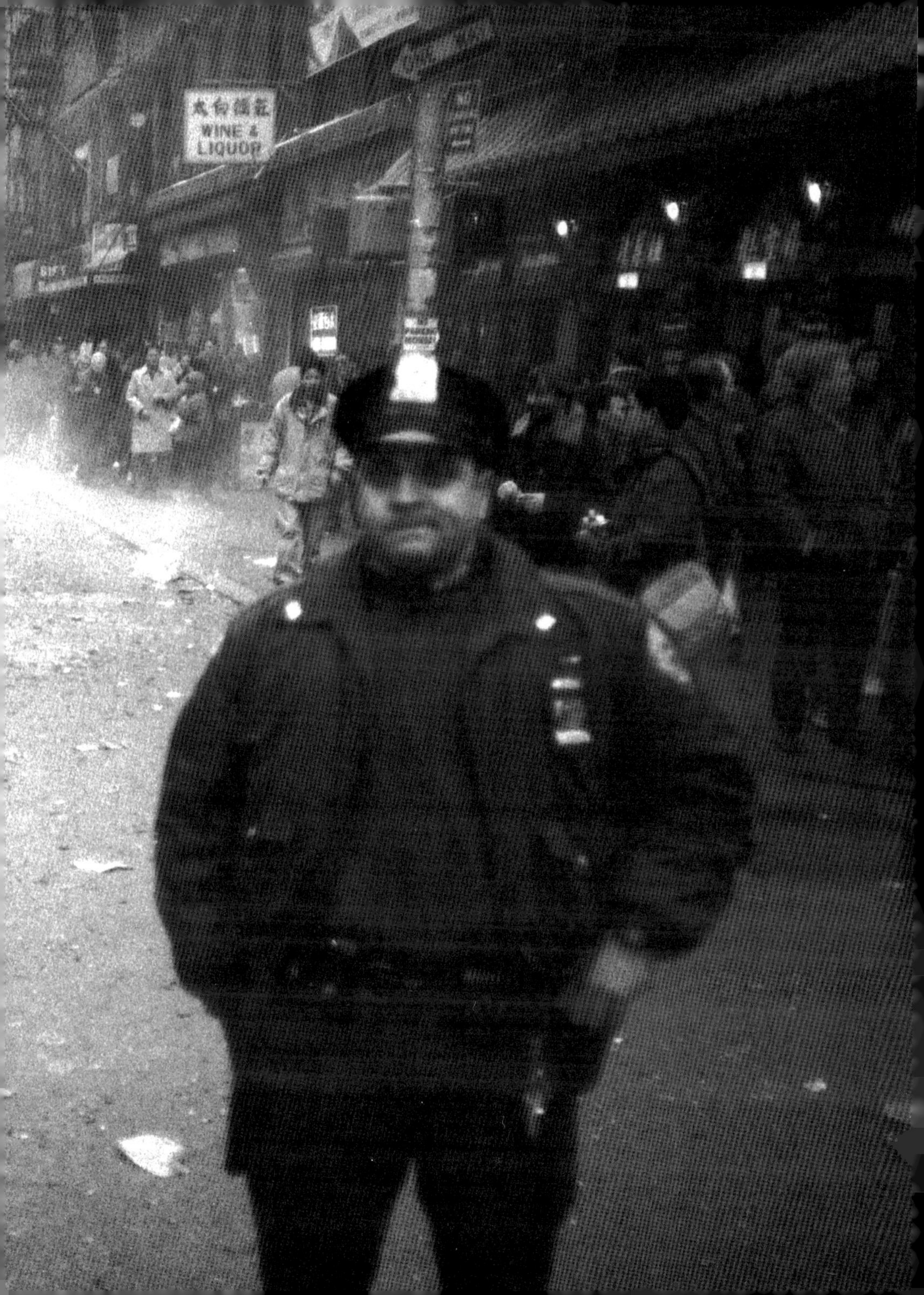

花福台太
WINE &
LIQUOR

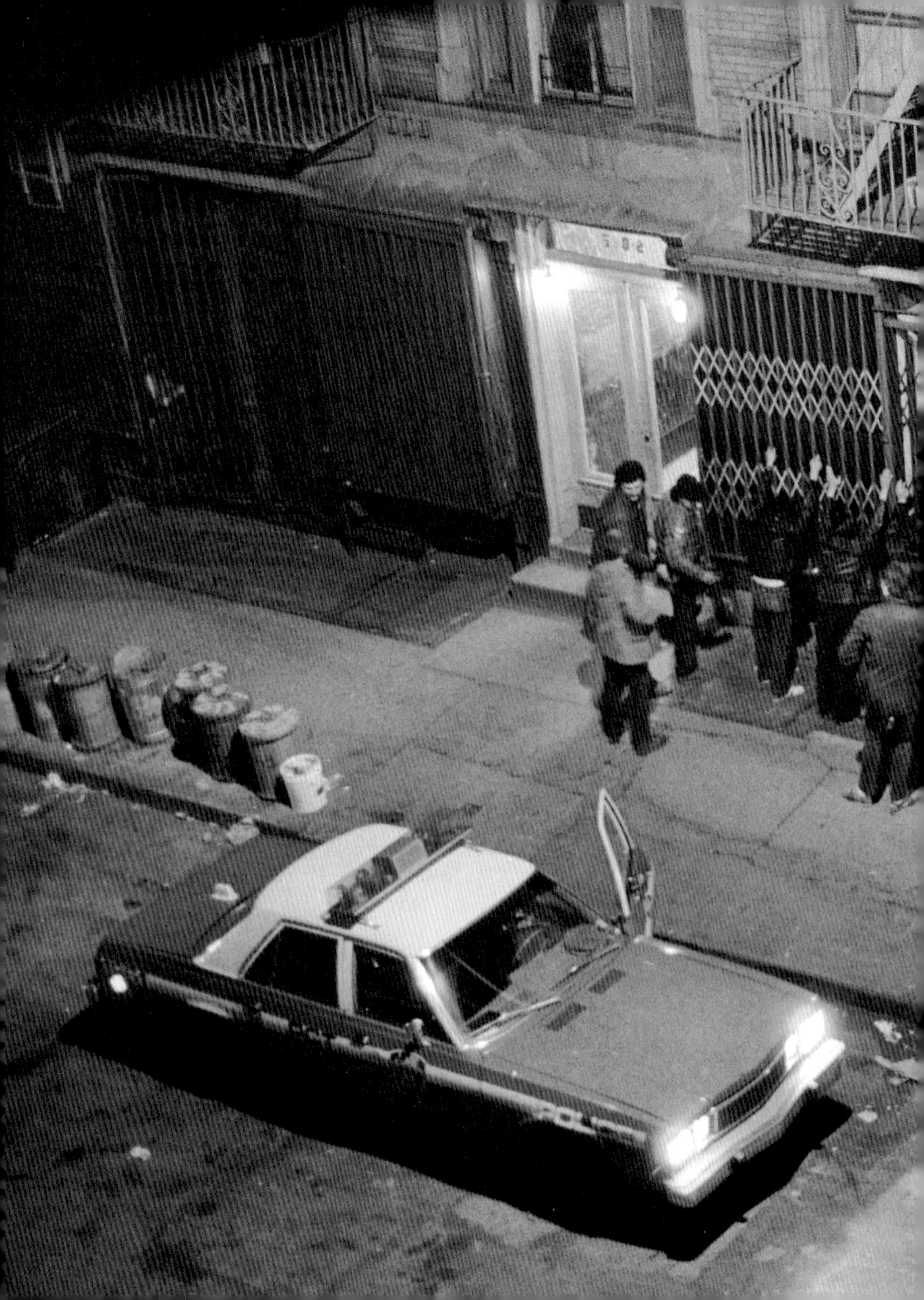